TEOTIHUACAN

HISTORY, ART AND MONUMENTS

Stone funeral mask covered with turquoise, shell and obsidian.

Cover:
Pyramid of the Moon
Photograph: Michael Calderwood

Text: Susana Vogel

Photographs:
Bonechi Archives
Michael Calderwood

◀▲ IINAIHI ❀ **CONACULTA**
Reproducción autorizada por el
Instituto Nacional de Antropología e Historia

Translation by: David B. Castledine

© 1995 by Monclem Ediciones, S.A. de C.V.
Leibnitz 31, Col. Anzures 11590
México, D.F., México
monclem@monclem.com
Tel.: 52 55 47 67

Printed in Mexico
Impreso en México
ISBN 968-6434-54-2

CONTENTS

Carved stone funerary mask. The horizontal bands denote the person's social position.

Teotihuacan Culture

Some 40 kilometers NE of Mexico City in a valley belonging to the central basin of Mexico lies the archaeological city of Teotihuacan. Its climate was originally temperate and semidry on the plains and semihumid on the surrounding higher ground, with rain from July to September. There were some lakes and caves that were used as religious centers.

The city was inhabited from 100 B.C. until 700 A.D. Its name is a Nahuatl word meaning "place of the gods" and was probably given to it later, or it may be a translation of the original name which has been lost in time since we do not know what language the original inhabitants spoke. Some experts suggest that they were Otomis, others believe they were Nahua-Chichimecs, and yet others relate them to the Olmec-Chochopopolocas. However the most widely accepted theory is that they belonged to a proto-Nahua group.

In the beginning the economy was based on agriculture, supplemented by hunting, fishing and gathering. Later there were social changes due to a population increase

Figure in "fine orange" pottery figure of a ballgame player wearing a hip protector.

and the storage of production surpluses which led not only to a division of work and to trade but also the centralization of power and permanent settlement, culminating in the construction of the great urban center.

Teotihuacan had systems for utilizing underground water and collecting rain, drains, artisans' workshops, dwelling complexes, markets, streets, temples, palaces, a large ceremonial center and districts where members of other Mesoamerican groups lived who had moved into the city. It was possible to build the large structures thanks to the numerous work force available and the priestly class. The latter, in addition to performing ceremonies and rites organized work and were in control of politics, administration and the economy. This was the social stratification and the division of productive labor.

Clay mask with a stylized butterfly under the nose symbolizing fire.

The activities of the inhabitants of the great city included agriculture, building, carving bone and shell, trade or exchange both with distant areas and in the city market, pottery, stone cutting, sculpture, painting and weaving textiles for clothes. Teotihuacan's influence, to be seen in pottery and architecture, spread along the trade routes to other regions in Mesoamerica, for example to the city of Tikal in Guatemala.

Religion occupied a position of prime importance, and the gods worshiped were associated with water, the earth and fertility. They included Tlaloc, the god of Rain, Chalchiutlicue, the goddess of Water, and Quetzalcoatl, the Feathered Serpent. The gods show the basic religious preoccupations of the Teotihuacanos and were represented in sculptures, clay figurines and mural paintings.

The decline of Teotihuacan began in the 7th. century A.D. and it was gradually abandoned until in the following century it lay completely empty, surrounded only by a few villages. It is not known exactly what led to this fall although there are several theories about it. These include a

Clay vessel with the head of a mythical bird and shell decorations on the body.

Monumental sculpture representing one of Teotihuacan's major deities: Chalchiutlicue, the goddess of Water.

*Funerary urn and incense burner where the remains
of cremated bodies were deposited. The lid is
decorated with a Quetzal-Butterfly figure.*

*Figurine in green serpentine
wearing a headdress, ear
spools and loincloth.*

famine caused by droughts which forced the inhabitants
to migrate; an intense struggle for power that divided the
ruling class; invasion by other groups from the north; a
popular uprising against the rulers, or some combination
of these possible causes, since archaeological explorations
have discovered traces of a fire which destroyed several
buildings on the Avenue of the Dead.

After it fell Teotihuacan became a place of pilgrimage for
other later peoples who went there to perform ceremonies honoring the gods. This was because according to le-
gend it was here that the Fifth Sun had been created which
lit the world in which the heirs of the Teotihuacan cul-
ture lived.

CHRONOLOGY OF TEOTIHUACAN
BASED ON THE DIFFERENT STYLES OF POTTERY

YEARS	PERIODS, AFTER VARIOUS EXPERTS	PERIODS, AFTER I.N.A.H.
1000		
950		
900	XOMETLA	COYOTLATELCO
850		
800	OXTOTICPAC	PROTO-COYOTLATELCO
750		
700	METEPEC	TEOTIHUACAN IV
650	XOLALPAN (late)	TEOTIHUACAN III-A
600		
550		
500	XOLALPAN (early)	TEOTIHUACAN III
450		
400	TLAMIMILOLPA (late)	TEOTIHUACAN II-A AND III
350		
300		
250	TLAMIMILOLPA (early)	TEOTIHUACAN II-A
200	MICCAOTLI	TEOTIHUACAN II
150		
100 A. D.	TZACUALLI (late)	TEOTIHUACAN I-A
50	TZACUALLI (early)	TEOTIHUACAN I
0		
50	PATLACHIQUE	PROTO-TEOTIHUACAN
100		
150	TEZOYUCA	CUICUILCO
200 B. C.		

ESSENTIAL CHARACTERISTCS OF TEOTIHUACAN'S CHRONOLOGICAL STAGES

XOMETLA. Remainders of some Teotihuacano groups with a floating population of villagers living in the half-ruined and abandoned city. Other sites that had been satellites of Teotihuacan show commercial and political growth.

OXTOTICPAC. Internal conflicts and attacks from the outside cause the groups in power to decline and leave the city.

METEPEC. Internal problems caused by over-population in the City-State, which could not grow without affecting agricultural land. External problems in the settlements subject to tribute and colonization by Teotihuacan.

XOLALPAN. Remodelling of city buildings to accommodate the flourishing economy; certain political and religious practices expressed in mural paintings. External expansion of the State.

TLAMIMILOLPA. Consolidation of Teotihuacan as a Governing State controlling the economic, political and religious system. Further building in the four quarters of the city organized as interdependent units of the State.

MICCAOTLI. Geometric plan established as part of extensive city planning. Buildings added to the Sun and Moon Pyramids.

TZACUALLI. Ceremonial area expanded as far as the Temple of Quetzalcoatl. Final building stage of the Sun and Moon Pyramids.

PATLACHIQUE. Creation of a communal Ceremonial Center (Sun and Moon Pyramids begun), drawing together the various populations neighboring on the valley.

TEZOYUCA. Concentrated settlements scattered over the sides of the valley which was used as agricultural land.

Monuments and art at Teotihuacan

Inside view of the Citadel showing its extent and layout.

The Citadel

This is a large quadrangle which the first Spaniards to visit the site named "Ciudadela" as it reminded them of a fortress because of the central building or "castle" from which ran a wall surrounding a court with one stepped entrance. Explorations made in the 20th century have revealed that the building was the Temple of Quetzalcoatl and that the

"wall" is made up of platforms 7 meters high with pyramidal structures on the top.

Studies have also shown that these buildings once had
small temples where festivals and ceremonies were held.
More recent investigations have discovered two buildings
t the sides of the Temple of Quetzalcoatl that seem to
ave been used as housing for the ruling class. Inside the
Citadel there is a sunken court and a square platform with
a staircase on each side and, to the southeast, an asymme-
rical structure built in seven superimposed stages.

Temple of Quetzalcoatl

This was built in two different periods. First was the structure decorated with high and low reliefs on the talud-tablero walls of the seven levels of the pyramid which were
built between 1 and 200 A.D. The decoration, unique on the
site, contains striking sculptures of feathered serpents
which possibly symbolize Quetzalcoatl himself, alterna-
ting with the god Tlaloc and the mythical *cipactli* or crocodile that symbolizes the fusion of earth and water, or
fertile land.

The second stage, dating to between 200 and 450 A.D.
completely covered the facade with the staircase on it and
also the relief carvings on the stages at the sides. This was
done to raise another pyramid structure in four stories

Serpent head surrounded by symbols representing the splashing of water as feather garlands.

The Temple of Quetzalcoatl with its decoration of the water serpent and the earth monster.

with plain talud and tablero walls, perhaps to hide the luxurious decoration of the preceding stage.

It was also during this period that the vast square known as the Citadel was built which encloses both the new and old Temple of Quetzalcoatl, and buildings were added at the sides.

While new explorations were being made the graves of warriors sacrificed in offering were discovered, the bodies with their hands behind their backs as if they had been tied. They were wearing ear-spools of green stone, shell-bead necklaces and elaborate pectorals and were accompanied by human figurines and obsidian articles such as projectile points and blades.

The Avenue of the Dead with the Pyramid of the Moon and the Cerro Gordo to the north.

Avenue of the Dead

Teotihuacan developed because of the great projects of urban infrastructure undertaken by the inhabitants. They built the N-S highway known as the Avenue of the Dead, (*Miccaotli* in Nahuatl) which runs for 2 km. from the Pyramid of the Moon to the Citadel and then continues south for a further 3 km.

This 40 m. wide road was interrupted by the Citadel Square and the Great Complex which housed the market. The streets running parallel to the avenue separated the city into districts and suburbs that spread to the four cardinal points.

On the stretch between the Ciudadela and the Pyramid of the Moon there is a masonry bridge replacing the original one over the San Juan river. This northern part of the avenue consists of 5 or 6 plazas with large staircases between them compensating for the rise of the terrain, until it reaches a slight slope down to the Pyramid of the Moon. The first plaza contains the Superimposed Buildings whose oldest structure had a decorated talud-tablero wall and the risers of the stairs were painted with *chalchi-huites*. In another section there is a talud-tablero wall with a buttress and a small wall topped with merlons. At the same level a wide overlaid staircase led to a small temple that was destroyed in the last building stage. The construc-tions on the upper part include groups with three pyra-midal base platforms that have staircases covering the older buildings.

Groups which originally stood around the East Plaza were destroyed by the builders of the coaching road between the villages of San Juan and San Martin de los Piramides who used stones from them to correct the different levels. The overlying levels of the West Plaza were noticed when restoration work was being done which revealed two pla-zas with small temples dating from different periods. The

Model of the buildings with two tiers and central staircase found along the Avenue of the Dead.

The long Avenue of the Dead with the Sun and Moon Pyramids.

Mural painting on the Avenue of the Dead of a puma on a vertical wall decorated with water motifs and a frieze of chalchihuites.

ramps of the oldest staircase end in the head of a serpent, and those of the more recent one finish with the head of a feline.

The buildings standing along almost 2 km. of the avenue all have a very similar architectural profile, due to the talud-tablero design typical of Teotihuacan, although each one has its own particular features. The Temple of Agriculture has a different look because when the later buildings were taken down during explorations at the end of the last century the first building stages were revealed that pre-date the classic talud-tablero style. In the substructure of the adjoining building a chamber was discovered with whimsical mural paintings that were named "Mythological Animals". On the other side of the Avenue there is a wall that incorporates a slab painted with a feline surrounded by waves.

The Mythological Animals mural with its water, serpent and feline motifs decorated the Temple of Agriculture.

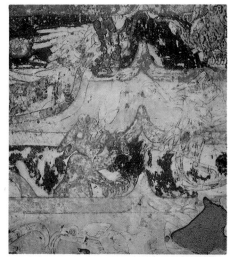

Group of the four-tiered buildings that border the Plaza of the Moon.

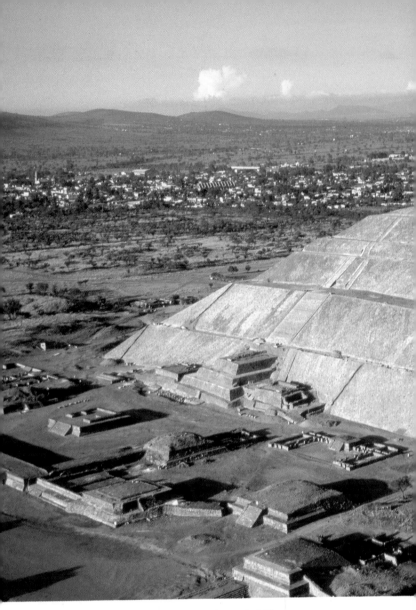

The Pyramid of the Sun, its plaza with the central Altar and different buildings on the Avenue of the Dead.

Pyramid of the Sun

Originally this consisted of four tiers standing on a square base measuring 200 m. along each side, although today there are five levels due to the rebuilding carried out bet-

ween 1905 and 1910. The pyramid is 60 m. high, without taking into account the small temple which used to stand on top and housed a stone idol that Archbishop Zumárraga ordered to be torn down in Colonial times.

At the sides of the staircases on the rear part there are large buttresses and inset stones for retaining the covering of tamped gravel overlaid with stucco painted red and white. This great monument is built with "boxes" of *tepetate* rock filled with earth and adobe to form the core, which was then covered with volcanic rock *(tezontle)*. Construc-

The monumental staircase of the Pyramid of the Sun.

tion was in two stages: between 0 and 200 A.D. the great pyramidal mass was raised and later the pyramid covering the central staircase of the west face, which also has four talud-tablero stories.

A natural cave was discovered under the center of the staircase during the 70s with a tunnel that runs for almost 100 m. into the center of the Pyramid and ends in four chambers where various archaeological objects were found.

Pyramid of the Moon and the buildings attached to it.

Pyramid of the Moon

This stands in the northern part of the city and by its shape imitates the Cerro Gordo whose Nahuatl name, *Tenan*, means "mother (or) protector of stone". It is the largest construction at Teotihuacan after the Pyramid of the Sun, covering an earlier building, and already had its present shape in the period 0 to 200 A.D.

Between 200 and 450 A.D. a structure was added to it with four talud-tablero tiers, opposite the staircase leading to the Avenue of the Dead. This had a platform at the top where ceremonies were performed in honor of Chalchiutlicue, the goddesss of Water, associated with the moon, to whom the top temple was dedicated and whose statue was found at the foot of the pyramid.

In front of the pyramid is the Plaza of the Moon which has an altar in the middle and a curious building with divisions inside. It is formed of four rectangular tiers and four on the diagonal, giving what is known as the "Teotihuacan cross".

Pyramid of the Moon and its plaza with a central Altar.

26

Porticoed court of the Quetzal-Papalotl Palace with merlons and pillars decorated with relief carvings. The original drainage outlet is in the floor.

Palace of Quetzal-Papalotl

This building stands next to others that seem to be part of it but in fact belong to earlier stages and were reused later. The pillars of the palace are decorated with carved figures of the mythical Quetzal-Mariposa (Quetzal-Butterfly) bird from which it takes its name. It has a rectangular inner patio surrounded by porticoes on its four sides that give access to rooms whose roofs were reconstructed because they were lost in a fire.

Where the interior patio and the east portico come together there is an entrance into the great antechamber, which can be reached from the Plaza de la Luna up a wide staircase. At the north end of this same portico another doorway leads to a group of smaller chambers on a lower level. The great staircase that connects with the Plaza de la Luna also leads to a smaller adjoining antechamber from which there is access to the west buildings.

The bird figure known as Quetzal-Butterfly carved on the columns of the Quetzal-Papalotl Palace has obsidian eyes and is surrounded by symbols of water and fire.

Palace of the Jaguars

This is an open section with superimposed buildings that were used at different periods. A pyramidal structure with talud-tablero stories that juts onto the plaza served as the base for a small temple with staircases and ramps in the shape of rattlesnakes.

One part of the palace is formed by the porticoes of the north building and the remains of structures surrounding the plaza. In the rooms with porticoes there are sloping walls decorated with felines with seashells on their flanks, blowing feathered conch shells.

The structures at the sides of the north building and those that face west and close the plaza contain pictures of jaguars covered with nets lying in the arms of a female torso wearing a *quechquemitl*.

Court of the Palace
of the Jaguars.

Puma with a feather
headdress and its back
covered with shells
playing a feathered
conch shell.

Temple of the Feathered Conches

This must have been built before the Palace of Quetzal-Papalotl because when the Palace was first used the other building was already in ruins and covered by another construction. A walkway connects the two monuments, and in the inner space where the Temple of the Feathered Conches was found there is access to the walls that give the building its name: the pillars are decorated with bands of feathered conches surrounded by friezes and jambs with flowers.

The platform joined to the temple has the classic Teotihuacan talud-tablero combination on three sides while the western front is interrupted by a staircase. On this there is the painting of a parrot watering a flower from its beak, a motif that is repeated on the inner sides of the vertical walls. There was once an altar at the center of this Great Plaza which in the first period was shared by both the Temple and the Palace of the Jaguars.

Facade of the Temple of the Feathered Conches on a talud-tablero platform.

Mural painting of a parrot with water flowing from its beak to water a flower. Temple of the Feathered Conches.

Tepantitla

This dwelling complex underwent alterations to its architecture and pictorial content in the course of time. Some walls were uncovered in the 40s that formed a room with an exit to two chambers decorated with paintings identified as representing Tlalocan or the Paradise of Tlaloc because of the festivities, games and amusements shown on the talud of the east wall. The figure of a god wearing a bird of prey as a headdress, with his arms open and large drops of water falling from his hands is repeated symmetrically. Above this figure is a leafy plant with flowers, birds and butterflies. Next to the figure of Tlaloc a priest is sowing

Detail of the mural showing a butterfly hunt. Palace of Tepantitla.

Elaborately dressed sower priest carrying a bag from which he takes seeds to scatter with his other hand.

seeds, while on the sloping wall people swim and play different games with balls. The mural on the NE wall shows a ballgame being played on a large court bounded by dismountable stelae similar to a target found in the La Ventilla area.

Beyond the entrance separating the Tlalocan wall and the ballgame wall there is a room where the murals show the "Procession of the Sower Priests", richly dressed figures, and the head of a crocodile adorned with feathers and with different motifs emerging from its leg representing a plea to the god for fertile land.

Tetitla

This is an example of the way structures were built over various times at different stages of Teotihuacan's period of splendor. In the first phase there were three small buildings separated by narrow streets; later the buildings grew and walls were demolished to join the housing areas together.

Among the architectural remains there are rooms with porticoes bounding plazas and patios, drains inside rooms, and at the center of the largest plazas there are altars and mural paintings where different styles and motifs are combined.

On the walls of the group there are falcons with blood flowing from their beaks, and the portico is decorated with a figure of the "Jade Goddess" with her back turned, her arms open and precious objects springing from her hands.

Hawk or falcon with a red torrent flowing from its beak, probably connected with sacrifice.

Deity wearing a jade mask, an elaborate headdress and elegant clothes with different jade-colored symbols emerging from his hands.

Teotihuacan

Mural painting in the White Patio of Atetelco showing a feline in a net wearing a feather headdress and eating a human heart. The volute coming from its mouth symbolizes roaring.

Reconstruction of an altar in the shape of a three-tiered stepped pyramid in the painted Patio of Atetelco

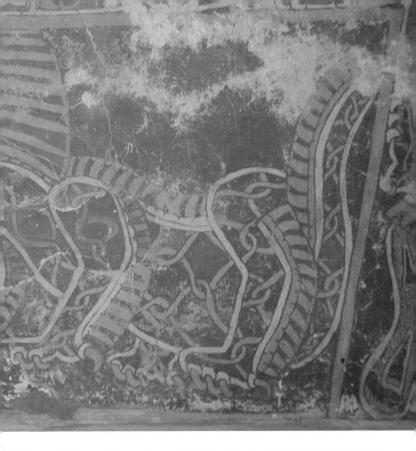

Atetelco

This is a major dwelling complex composed of several sections including the Painted Patio, where an altar was built, and the White Patio, decorated with interesting murals.

In portico 1 is the painting of a feline covered with a net; on the vertical walls is a net with the head of a feline hanging from it and, in the spaces, the head of a coyote with human features. The sloping wall of portico 2 has a feline caught in a net and a coyote, both wearing feather headdresses, and on the vertical walls there is a human figure wearing a bird of prey headdress, all designed with originality.

Portico 3 has on the talud a person performing a ritual dance; the vertical wall shows an anthropomorphic bird in warrior costume and at the side of the portico there is the painting of a person with his feet turned inward.

Entrance with steps to the Zacuala complex which has spacious rooms inside.

Entrance to the dwelling complex of Yayahuala.

Zacuala and Yayahuala

Zacuala is an elegant dwelling complex with rooms, porticoes, patios, a central plaza and antechambers with drains that were connected to the street-drain system that collected water. This supplemented the urban communication system.

The dwelling complex of Yayahuala is surrounded by a wall and bounded by streets, one of them linked to the street-drain system. A staircase leads to the antechamber of the sunken plaza which is connected to three dwelling or religious and administrative complexes. It contains buildings with porticoes, corridors and the remains of a smaller entrance.

View of the Museum, with the Pyramid of the Sun in the background.

The Museum

The Museum stands at the center of the archaeological site of Teotihuacan, close to the Pyramid of the Sun.
The entrance hall is decorated with a stone slab carved in relief with one of Teotihuacan's most important deities, associated with water, earth and fertility. The rooms display samples of the raw materials employed on the site, explanations as to how the environment was managed, examples of architecture and various arts such as pottery, bone carving, painting and stonecutting, information on Teotihuacan's vision of the universe and its religion, the symbolism of murals, funeral masks, and urns that contained the ashes of the cremated. In addition, as an example of the

Funeral mask in serpentine with stereotyped Teotihuacano features.

rites performed when the temple of Quetzalcoatl was begun, there is the collective burial of nine male and four female sacrificial victims that was discovered at one side of the temple.

The main room has a glass floor so that visitors can walk over a scale model of the city to appreciate its grandeur and gain an overall picture of the archaeological site. The effect is rounded off by a large window looking out onto the Pyramid of the Sun.

"Fine orange" ware vessel decorated with a fork-tongued feline wearing a feather headdress.

Above. Stone statue of the old god of Fire, Huehueteotl, with a brazier on his head.

43

Pottery vessel covered with a layer of stucco beautifully painted with the god Tlaloc.

Hollow clay figure of a man sitting cross-legged with a vessel in each hand, possibly as a symbol of offering.

Offering-burial group from the Temple of Quetzalcoatl. The sacrificial victims were found half-bending with their hands tied behind their backs.

Clay incense burner in the shape of a skull probably used in funeral ceremonies.

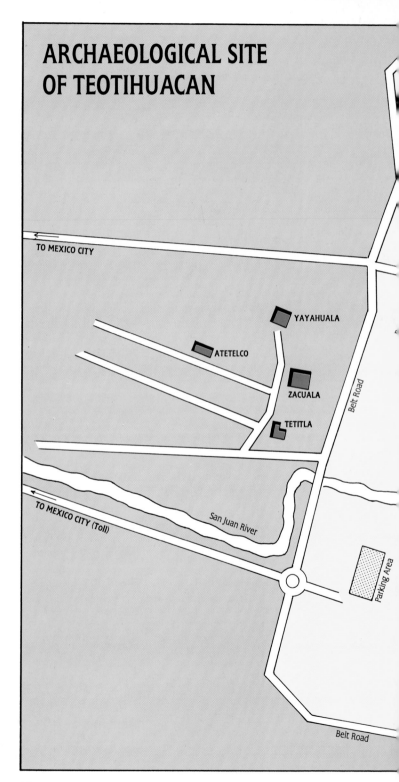

ARCHAEOLOGICAL SITE OF TEOTIHUACAN

TO MEXICO CITY

YAYAHUALA

ATETELCO

ZACUALA

TETITLA

Belt Road

TO MEXICO CITY (Toll)

San Juan River

Parking Area

Belt Road

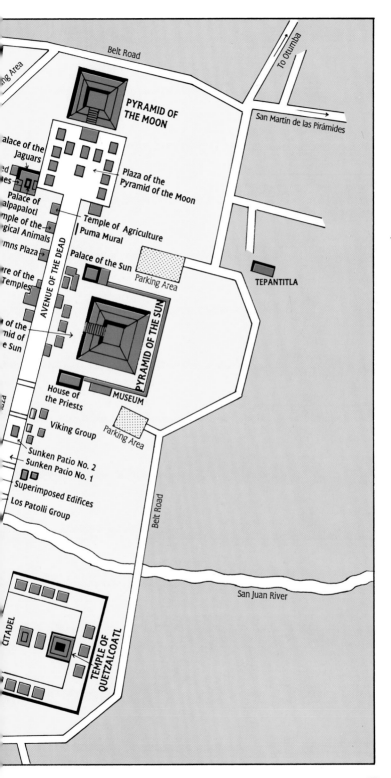

Belt Road

To Otumba

San Martín de las Pirámides

PYRAMID OF THE MOON

alace of the Jaguars

Plaza of the Pyramid of the Moon

Palace of alpapalotl

mple of the gical Animals

Temple of Agriculture

Puma Mural

mns Plaza

AVENUE OF THE DEAD

Palace of the Sun

Parking Area

TEPANTITLA

re of the Temples

of the mid of e Sun

PYRAMID OF THE SUN

House of the Priests

MUSEUM

Viking Group

Parking Area

Sunken Patio No. 2
Sunken Patio No. 1
Superimposed Edifices
Los Patolli Group

Belt Road

San Juan River

CITADEL

TEMPLE OF QUETZALCOATL

47

Printed in:
Repeticiones Gráficas, S.A. de C.V.
Pacífico 312, Col. Rosedal, Coyoacán
04330 - México, D.F., March, 2003